Sometimes a Screech Owl
Ridire Quinn

Sometimes a Screech Owl ©2018 by **Ridire Quinn**. Published in the United States by Vegetarian Alcoholic Press. Not one part of this work may be reproduced without expressed written consent from the author. For more information, please contact vegalpress@gmail.com

Acknowledgements

I would like to thank the following publications in which these poems appeared, sometimes in slightly different versions.

Burdock Magazine: "come…," "(L)earning Breath,"

Five 2 One Magazine: "Yellowing" (The section on Cleaning Pearls is quoted from "Henley's Twentieth Century Formulas, Recipes And Processes," by Norman W. Henley, Copyright 1916, The Norman W. Henley Publishing Company)

Fox Adoption Magazine: "A Campfire Song or, What I Did for Summer Vacation"

Great: Poems of Resistance and Fortitude: "Baptism"

Harbinger Asylum: "Regenesis"

In Want of Jasmine: "Comfort"

Return to the Gathering Place of the Waters: "adam, made of silt," "*and i carry…*," "A Drier World," "(dis)course," "

Silvae Magazine: "Alleyways," "Passages"

The wild beasts of the desert shall also meet with the wild beasts of the island, and the satyr shall cry to his fellow; the screech owl also shall rest there, and find for herself a place of rest. - Isiah 34:14 (King James Version)

but,

Wildcats shall meet with hyenas, goat-demons shall call to each other; there too Lilith shall repose, and find a place to rest. - Isaiah 34:14 (NSRV)

Exodus Inherited

1	Alleyways
2	Exodus Inherited
3	Passages
4	Yellowing
8	Sometimes a Screech Owl, Part One
9	A Drier World
11	A Campfire Song or, What I Did for Summer Vacation
13	Drier Gods

Regenesis

16	*come...*
18	Neon
19	*Sing(ing)...*
20	*and i carry...*
22	Baptism*
23	Sometimes a Screech Owl, Part Two
24	(L)earning Breath
27	Regenesis

Paradise Abandoned

31	A Nail and a Cross
32	Paradise Abandoned
33	What We Miss
34	(dis)course
35	*teeth...*
36	Sometimes a Screech Owl, Part Three
37	*When S(h)allow...*
39	adam, made of silt

Among All the Bloody Things

43	Among All the Bloody Things
44	Belittle
45	Mirrors
46	Crane
47	Sometimes a Screech Owl, Part Four
48	babylon, diligent
49	Tamar
50	Eve, of the Harsher Parts of Dawn

Epilogue
53   Sometimes a Screech Owl, Part Five

I would like to thank everyone who ever held a mirror for me.

I dedicate this book to the force of nature who is my son, Louren.

EXODUS INHERITED

alleyways

running through
(the secret
black
alley)ways that
stray un-
seen throughround
this city(bleached
harsh-
white by the sun's relent-
less passing)that veil be-

hind
marble restroom
walls,
under mosaic foyers or
aside
(three-in-the)morning-stained

coffee mugs(you
can see them if you
look just so, just right,
under old and yellowed light,
under more honest light),

you carry words
that you desperately
need to deliver, words

that breed in
the creases of your brain(growing
suddenly immense and
populous)until the
megrim pressure
nudges the wish that you
would scream louder(if only
someone could hear you),

the walls drenched
with echoing mural.

Exodus Inherited

The strong, raging river of my
birth, several promised lands
away, I can smell its waters.

      (but where is
the Sacred Tree
        foretold in our
Father's dream?)

Sun-skinned, tongues filling
our mouths, the desire for water
overwhelming the memory of it.

      (This is no river!
      This is a stream,
      a rivulet,
      a mirage.)

Pouring over elementary school text-
books for just the right nomenclature,
forgetting the water ever existed.

      (We miss the
desert: we
knew when the
sun would rise.)

You had asked me for rain, accused
me when it flooded. This
rise of inevitable waters.

Passages

I miss walls
if only for the secret spaces
behind them, giving
sneak and

subtle
when doors and foyers just won't
do. The slated
framework

leeches light from
chandeliered interior into
this narrow-way,
this evasion of thoroughfares.

No room to dance but
rather to creep along, along,
to peer out
away from intimacy.

Along those lamp-lit hallways
that the ghosts travel,
how can I breathe?
Who do I talk to when I

find myself on the
other side of the room?

Yellowing

i've got this poem now
relating a memory i had of
the Polaroid I took of this pearl i
once found.

it's all that i have.

that's not quite true:
i also have a yellowing copy of
*Henley's Twentieth Century
Formulas, Recipes and Processes.*

it was given to me by my mother.

it warns that pearls(too)
yellow over time.
by absorbing perspiration
from being worn in the hair, at
the throat, and on
the arm.

this poem i have(now. that
i wrote?)
tells me that i
never had the pearl.
I only took a picture of it(leaving
it where i found it),
put the Polaroid in my pocket to
carry around with me(to
to help me remember
its beauty).

*Henley's Formulas, Recipes
and Processes*. and
the Polaroid of a pearl.

they were all that i had.

the Henley's was yellowing from age
(does the poem mention

that? i don't remember). the Polaroid was just starting to, around the edges, from absorbing perspiration(from being remembered).

Cleaning Pearls[1]

Pearls turn yellow in the course of time by absorbing perspiration on account of being worn in the hair, at the throat, and on the arms. There are several ways of rendering them white again.

I
The best process is said to be to put the pearls into a bag with wheat bran and to heat the bag over a coal fire, with constant motion.

II
Another method is to bring 8 parts each of well-calcined, finely powdered lime and wood charcoal, which has been strained through a gauze sieve, to a boil with 500 parts of pure rain water, suspend the pearls over the steam of the boiling water until they are warmed through, and then boil them in the liquid for 5 minutes, turning frequently. Let them cool in the liquid, take them out, and wash off well with clean water.

III

---

[1] The section on Cleaning Pearls is quoted from
Henley's Twentieth Century Formulas, Recipes and Processes
Author Norman W. Henley
Copyright 1916, The Norman W. Henley Publishing Company

Place the pearls in a piece of fine linen, throw salt on them, and tie them up. Next rinse the tied-up pearls in lukewarm water until all the salt has been extracted, and dry them at an ordinary temperature.

IV
The pearls may also be boiled about 1/4 hour in cow's milk into which a little cheese or soap has been scraped; take them out, rinse off in fresh water, and dry them with a clean, white cloth.

V
Another method is to have the pearls, strung on a silk thread or wrapped up in thin gauze, mixed in a loaf of bread of barley flour and to have the loaf baked well in an oven, but not too brown. When cool remove the pearls.

VI
Hang the pearls for a couple of minutes in hot, strong, wine vinegar or highly diluted sulphuric acid, remove, and rinse them in water. Do not leave them too long in the acid, otherwise they will be injured by it.

the poem doesn't explain
what happened to the Polaroid of
the pearl. only that it was supposed to
help me remember beauty.
i really don't remember ever
having it. the only
thing i can say
is that my pockets
are empty.

that's not quite true:
i can say that my clothes smell of vinegar.
the milk tastes like soap.

i read in the poem that
i held on to the memory of the Polaroid
for a long time. it was all that i had.

i sometimes wonder what happened to
Henley's Formulas, and Processes,
but i don't really want to know. i think
i wear it around my neck, a comforting
oppression, but i can't see it.

maybe it's that i simply don't
think about it anymore.

what I do think about is that
the poem is beginning to turn yellow.
i no longer have the paper
it was written on.it's the poem
itself.turning yellow.i carry it
around
to(keep it safe)remember the Polaroid.

it's all that i have now.

i don't know
if any of it is true

but i think i.wrote it: this poem of
a me(mory)i had.of this
Polaroid.i once.

found.

Sometimes a Screech Owl
Part One

That's no Queen's drink, say
        A Queen's drink is what the Queen says it is, the
the Courtiers.
                              Courtesans whisper.
The Queen should not make such a face.
                                  What face is that?
The face of a whore in resilient sensation.
                                Is not the Queen this, too?

A Drier World

Desiccation
is a new word
I found. I
like this word.

Desiccation
is a drier word.
A desert word.
A deserted word

that leaves behind
glossy pamphlets
promoting a motel's
swimming pool

and your father's
umbrella, unused and
leaning in the
dark corner by the back door.

I would like to
find a drier
wor(l)d

where all umbrellas are left leaning
and pamphlets are the primary form of literature.

Either will do.

We're too wet, you say.
We sweat
just getting up
off the couch. We leave
stains on the leather.
Aren't we
wet enough with
humidity and
rain forests
and condensation
and ocean

currents?

No. I am not wet enough.

A Campfire Song or, What I Did for Summer Vacation

The lyrics
are lost to childhood;
even the cold and yellow
light of
nostalgia cannot illuminate
them: that
campfire song,

or the
telephone number
she
wrote on your hand on
the last day,
that last, hot day
in August that only
compounded your
already sweaty
nervousness.

sweat does that. sweat
smears ink
just as easy as
it does all
those August days
into a
single
mass
of
sweltering
memory
when suddenly
you and she
are on different
busses,
too
young, too
stupid, too

thirteen to
understand why

your gut is screaming
the importance
of this goodbye, why
"see ya"
is as small and
insufficient

as trying to put out that campfire by peeing on it.

Fire still sings,
"a boy and a girl in a little canoe,"
while you stare
at your once-stained hand
in its flickering memory,
but you can never
remember if they ever
kissed
while that giant moon
shined on
and on.

drier gods

the scent on the wind,
hounds harp and
howl, straining at leashes.

it's the Wind
i'm after. an alter
to appease. a face
to curse. flesh to murder.

we build shelters
where
the torches
blow out, our eyes wild and
dry.

wilder hair revealing
(y)our beauty, the truth
behind clouds, how to
let go
of leashes in this
sober country.

REGENESIS

come...

come
my sweet
pucker up
and in puckering
so lead
as carriages
their horses

through
gated ways
of (un-)
guarded black-gloved footmen

slipping those
(very the same)
black gloves
into your corset
to away with the
jubilation that i had lent you
for just the one day:

from last midnight
until only tonight's mid-
night

but tomorrow knows
a 12:05 when it strikes!

why then this when
is the how you come to me?

your pocket watch
pleading an
11:55 case but clock towers
everywhere testifying on tomorrow's behalf

you're late

and you owe
me

a kiss

Neon

-1-
when I say I
love you(
mis-
trust you)
I am not
consum(at)ing your
worth: how can I
when
I've only ever known a
you-under-this-moon?
(there is only ever one
everything at any given
moment)
to him
you are only ever
you-under-that-sun(I've
never known this you)when
he tells you one can never
count on
moonlight, calls you
beautiful only at noon.
mo(ve)ments
(that)are
more about in-relation-to
than
in-
here(nt),
as much about
(co?)ordinates
as composition.
and you:
you will only meet
(y)our lovers
in the pre-dawn city as it
rains,
neon giving
lust(er) to sidewalks
in ways the moon or the sun
never could

-2-
Police sirens and rattling subway trains are hope for continued night, but in this mo(u)rning glare, the GIRLS-GIRLS-GIRLS sign outside your studio's third story window might as well be advertising stationery, its neon promise no longer providing proof of the temple that is the small of your back, so worshiped by rain and the tongue of (every)last night's lover.

Sing(e)(ing)...

Sing(e)(ing)
deeply: your skin.
tight tingling tight-
ly in oh
specifically
purposefully
directioned weals

wringing out
wetter aches,
earning belt
(or
maybe
rope
or even
flog)to keep knees parted
as your lips should be

t(h)rusting now sore
joInts
(and my hands?)
to keep your
hips up
(and so oh your pussy
where my lips can reach)

and i carry...

and i carry
you with me
in (y)ears and tongue
and try(
oh god must i try?) to
ignore
and ignore
these achingly long
ingly
fingertips.

they
are covered in
paper-cuts(even
though
i licked them
for traction)
rummaging through
stacks of old poetry
for some explanation of
wh(y)o(u)

but all i
found
but all you
showed me
but all we wrote
(will write)
was(is)be-
cause and effect
(formally, conditionally):

if you trust
(wh(y)ou)trust)
then you will trust
and it's all logic
except when it's lust
and then it's all
the more logic(ally
lustfully beauti)

fully
aware of shy(ly
obscene)
vulnerability
and exposure.

hovering
(before me)
i(reach
out)
behind you(r
behind) and
touch(pale)
skin
with now-healed
fingertips
(stacks of poetry
set aside for later
reading)
and empty,
open palms
that you blessed
with breathless
trust.

Baptism

Dragging hand-me-down virtues
through tunnels of
barbed wire, wrapping
ethic(and morality, some
times)inside oily rags
on the verge of igniting themselves.

we fight and
we spit
and we wild an-
d we spark,
fearful of being over-
heard by glass-walled neighbors:

our louder, American pastime
of digging in our back yards
at midnight for only the latest
psychologies, hoping they won't
calls the cops. no. we need
something aching, ancient.

pine and hemlock come to mind. and rites
that demand more blood and dance.

to fight and
to spit
and to wild an-
d to spark
is to dig in the back yards of
our ids and our egos regardless of
philosophy's agency.

there is no more time to
kneel before, only to rail
against, to lean and press
against, to fight-spit-wild-spark
against,

to share the splinters
from this, our baptism.

Sometimes a Screech Owl
Part Two

Thorns Her fortress, a drawbridge of nettles.
A court of hyenas, dragons, and of
ostritches and jackals. High
brambl'd towers. A night(ful)
Queen (sometimes a
screech owl) prays:

bring to me
an (ill)shining
(k)night, moonless(ly questing),
thirsty, that he might
speak to me a truth.

Her messengers went.
Into the wilderness they went, along
cobblestoned or
wheel-rutted roads they went,
and down thistl'd paths.

With all that they
were, their keen'd ears
and satyr'd laughter, what
they heard was:

The Queen
Seeks a Fool.

(L)earning Breath

we (l)earn our first breath
with a spank,

    [breathe]

wailing at the firm hand,
allowing it to resonate,
not yet knowing the words to keep
going further:

    [breathe]

more. please.

    [breathe]

these exhaled words
mirror, (rel)ease
us from apneic silences
parenthetically surrounding
being
(cal)led on or
calling after.

    [breathe]

more would have been enough;
please would have filled us,
but instead they impose
a name on us

    [breathe]

and give us first n(our)ishment from
mothers' breast milk. we
forget breathe,
learn consume.
breath becomes
a thing that lives outside moments,
becomes

baited
in(be)tween.

    [breathe]

this is how you come to me:
baited and living outside,
fighting to inhale,
frenzied to exhale,
unable to even cry(anymore)
or to beg
well enough to
choose your own name.

    [breathe]

you lean in(to
my firm hand),
but my words
demand that you
arch: *more. please.*

    [breathe]

you start to
remember h(ow)
to breathe,
to y(earn),
to beg:

    [breathe]

more. please.

    [breathe]

we (t)each ourselves
anticipation.

    [breathe]

we call each other
our by (h)our truer names.

    [breathe]

we learn together
what breathing finally means:

    [breathe]

rhythmic. resonating.
unrelenting.

    [breathe]

Regenesis

In the absence of a beginning, there is an After(which cannot be helped)and there is a Before(which is better anyway). In between(struggling to find breath), the Night-Dreamer soothes the screech owl's hands that've cramped from sulfuring a cabinets' rusty latches. Within these cabinets are plates fashioned by her other hands(her older hands, her hands from the Before). In the After, Jesters spin these plates on hand-sticks(made from her bones)for the entertainment of children(her children)playing in the sun. She'll glimpse them from beneath the basement stair, straining to touch their feet. Feet of iron and of tyranny, of sun and of clouds, of wind and of stone, her heart timed to their tantrumic marching. With night-time voices, they tell the other children their mother's stories. With brutal feet, they kill them when they question how such stories are to be told.

PARADISE ABANDONED

A Nail and a Cross

an old woman
steps out of
the past
   (she
pulls a nail
out of her
pocket)
     her eyes
closed, now, to the
cycling tides.

   she
reaches her arms
toward the sky
and a shadow
(now alien, now
distended, now dark)
sprouts wings, whispers
something like
sin.

   the
woman drives the
nail into the
sand, trying
   (to
tear away, trying)
to leave behind
the shadow now
pinned to the
earth.

Paradise Abandoned

you're not
(w)here
(you live,
my heart)

proximity (is?to?)
these fingernails and
(your
t)highs a lust:so retracted
i('ll be)

in eyes
cateract'd to un-
seeing you:blind i('ll
be)

so to hear
your song or cry or
moan in quiet(ing
ticks of seconds and
tocks of miles):in
deafness i('ll be)

in(haling) you(r)
(in)sobriety across
chasms:anosmic i('ll be)

leaving tongues as lust's desperate
diplomats

What We Miss

Before you're even gone,
The skies open up their mouths and spit our ardent harmonies;
the sidewalks develop new cracks from which concrete shards erupt;
all windows stop reflecting the sun's light.

My feet lose traction, a
fall that hands catch;
breathing stops; my eyes dry out while searching the cracks for what
I missed:

...the point you were trying to make, of caffeine free.

...the mark in my last poem, in the gift I sent.

...the call to arms, to speak now or to hold my peace.

...the deadline for submission, for finding you free.

...the last call, the last train.

I shut out
the skies and,
in the day's
final beams of
unreflected light, grope
among the cracks
and concrete shards
for the chance
I know I
won't find but
can't risk missing.

I watch my own light seep out through these
 labor stained hands now pricked with
  opaque slivers: new beams that reflect
   violently off the store windows on
    either side of the street. People start to gather, a
     yearning audience eager to join the skies'
      obsessive harmony. And I nearly miss it:
       under these lights, they are singing your name.

(dis)course

The urinal seems abnormally high. I
hope I'm not shrinking but back at our
table, I'm eye-level with water glasses.

I climb up into my seat. I want
to ask for a phone book but your
silence has taught the waitress to ignore

me, too. The diner is full of people.
People chewing. Like we're
chewing. As if everything is all right.

We continue. To chew. Long
past the final course. After all
the plates are cleared.

teeth...

teeth
chiseled
from granite
gnashing against
damnation's

fire: i taste sweat. the

salt
left behind by
bodies sweltering
in the wake of the
gravy train demands
to know the
love promised by
god.

Sometimes a Screech Owl
Part Three

Div-iners and dream readers,
Jug-glers and
dance-birds and
fell-tale-tellers,
sun-faeries and
switch fencers, gallows-dwarves
and hail tamers,
stone speakers, iron-wizards, rain merchants, the Lion-faced.
The Choler guilders.
Glass-eaters.

Turn and in turn
and by each by, every one

dismissed.

When S(h)allow

When s(h)allow,
uneven,
billowing down the
hard throats of
these deep caves,
expanding, so thinning:

This, my love, is my love.

Who hiding secret keepsakes,
the nooks and crannies
or
widening, unlit caverns and soundless pits only
guessed at
or
my threatening candle dangerous because
of unexposed pockets of methane:

You, my love, are my love.

Where dancing to mouths,
following hints of fresher air
but moving toward
more final horrors of
alone or lost, my
strained and bulging
eyes urging
your earth beneath:

Take my love; find, my love.

What these dim
lanterns, strung down other passages,
proving a previousness
I dare not follow:

Turning my love into my love.

Why in stale air you know my breath,
absorbing to

a spell cast
for further thinning
of my breath's moisture that others will breathe:

Inhale, my love. Exhale my love.

adam, made of silt

she('ll speak a delic)ate gravel

into your
hardened ear
on the day you sling in the towel:
                on the day
                you(r dick) declare(s)
                war on her lips.

behind those lips
you('ll find)
cement words that've been churning since
                your lacquered words made
                your bed seem appealing, made
                your bed seem a safer place
than her own suspended high
                above a doorman and his spirit
                and high
                above the street and its sp(ir)it,
                with its deeper,
                cognac-colored steam
                tunnels lit by lamps burning
                dimly of an angel('s fire)s

but then again,
you're You
and
she's She
and
now there's a grave
in the graveled dirt
just as pale and shallow as Lake Eerie (pre)tends to be
until the silted bottom suddenly drops out
                when you are far from shore,
                when you forget how to swim in a
Lake,
                when you find yourself wishing for an
ocean for no other reason than the salt,

would rather drown with

salt in your throat and salt in your lungs
than the sickly silt of a lake-floor that drops out
					when you are far from shore,
					when a serpent breathes the water,
					when your child finds murder.

AMONG ALL THE BLOODY THINGS

Among All the Bloody Things

Kukri moon slung low.
Yellowing. Ancient
moon. Aching at sharp angles,
a slice through thick atmosphere.

Wanting chant, wanting
ritual, wanting slow-flowing and deliberate
fabric. Suffering no other light

except deep, still waters.
She'll rage at the tides, forget she is the cause.

Tonight, she hates all cities: their stolen light,
their planes and their towers,
their time turned from the sun.

She cannot bathe in her own light.
Among all the lonely and wild and bloody things,
she cannot bathe in her own light:

> *I am not your hunter's bow. Or your maiden; not your*
> *pregnant or waxing divine.*
> *I am not the horns of your god. The sun does not pursue*
>
> *me. I am not your scimitar when you have no mirror for*
>
> *me. Fuck*
> *me. Then get out. Let*
> *me disappear beyond this horizon. Let*
> *me find curvature. Let*
> *me see a waning earth.*

Belittle

The phone rang.
Twice.
You picked up and
a voice spoke lies,
the words passing through you.

Your appetite swelled
as you watched
a fan slowly turn

You didn't know it,
but you were chewing on a pen:
the plastic conforming to
your bite.

With your toes,
you played the piano.

You drew a line up your
belly
and caressed your breast.

You sighed,
desperately.

Mirrors

my whiskey you
your wine me
overfilled with
lips dripping
over wet
chins-
blouses with
tale telling stains
moreprove an
eclipsed mid-
night than
fingerprints on
glasses or the
ghosts we leave behind
in bar mirrors

Crane

A crane, falling
through snow,
the winds ripped from her wings, crashing
into a garden.

Into THE garden.

as in:
"I'm headed out to
the garden!"
you might announce to the empty,
frameless hall.

What pictures there are
you had found in glossy magazines,
thumb-tacked to the plaster,
careful of the corners. Or
the postcard of the Eiffel Tower,
sent to yourself
so there would be mail
when you returned from
from the corner drug store.

There, among the cabbages and
Japanese eggplants,
the crane lay
broken, stoic,
blistered, quiet, and beaten,
there among the
cabbages and Japanese eggplants.

She suffered herself to be taken inside,
to be carried across a threshold,
to be found within walls and ceilings,
to heal.

Leaving the Wind unable to forgive
iron and sun, clouds, and unmoving stone.

Sometimes a Screech Owl
Part Four

She draws a line
in the dust on the floor.

Through the fleeing footprints, a line
in the dust on the floor.

A second line, then.
A third and another, rectangl'd
in the dust on the floor.

Ornate swirls.
Tilts and
flourishes at the corners, corners
she'll dance around, three times around erasing
the abandon'd footprints
in the dust on the floor.

An elaborate frame, drawn in the dust on the floor.

Moonless rain falls through
the cracked rafters, spatters
in the dust on the floor.

Reflection begins in the dust on the floor.

She works her fingers
into the dust and under the dust,
takes hold of the (ill)shining
frame emerging from
the dust on the floor.

Heavy, so heav(enl)y, this framed mirror is.
To lift,
to brace,
to let speak.

Babylon, diligent

Spiral d(own,
you)? Dig
in, or claw up, you
taking my dusty h(and
in the other,
a shovel,
blisters cracking
along the heart-line,
the hickory handle
bloody)and?

The gods whisp(
er no),
as do-
es Babylon, diligent
in her wild(er-
ness, with kindly)eyes that
tell you that wisdom and
angels wait for you out
past her hori-
zons.

Tamar

what begins
in rev(elry)
-olution ends with
Ab(solution)
-salom,whose words imprint
through her body's salt,
extracted from the
in(tended)
-voluntary
moisture of a Dawn that
took too long to come:
plumbing great flesh, and
greater flesh, crying out for
even greater flesh
while a father weeps only
for the son, splitting
a flooded earth
between spilled semen
and flowing blood.

Eve, of the Harsher Parts of Dawn

you are the
only deadly
thing above
(me killing)
me.

pressing me
to juiced pressings of
i/you, body
to
body

impressing we
the tall grass.

one, then two sets
of footprints heading to,
but only
one body shaped-impression
of(you in)me.

(the t)all grass tells
the b(l)ind sun of my arching
back, the lying
leaves of your arms around me.

we ask the bees and
the birds about the
birds-and-the-
bees and(t)each the world
how to populate,
so (l)earning how to die.

EPILOGUE

Sometimes a Screech Owl
Part Five

(n)one to (no)one
can breathe (y)our breath
(my love) insomuch
as you

when you reve(a)l
teeth: lips pulled
back to gritted
g(r)in at the first
sip of a martini,
your reflection
naked, an excess
of olives macerating.

www.ingramcontent.com/pod-product-compliance
Lightning Source LLC
Chambersburg PA
CBHW060506080526
44584CB00015B/1571